AUTOBLIVION

AUTOBLIVION

Trey
MOODY

CONDUIT BOOKS
& EPHEMERA

ISBN: 979-8-9883272-1-9

Published by Conduit Books & Ephemera
788 Osceola Avenue
Saint Paul, Minnesota 55105
www.conduit.org

Book design by Scott Bruno/b graphic design

Distributed by Small Press Distribution
www.spdbooks.org

Cover images: *[Oregon National Forest. Effect of fire on an old burn. Before fire there was a dense cover of green brush. Previous fire was about ten years before]; Children playing a singing game during afternoon play period at homestead school. West Virginia.* Courtesy the Library of Congress.

CONTENTS

3

for
Charlotte

I wish the idea of time would drain out of my cells and leave me quiet even on this shore.

—Agnes Martin

1

Some Circles

I could tell you anything I want—the saddest night

of my life I learned the magnolia

predates the bee, the flower's parts toughened

to withstand most any pollinating beetle.

I tell you this fact for no reason

other than it impressed me by making my own life

seem even sadder in the way I imagine

a walnut or an antique marble might feel

at the foot of a singular mountain. Like you, I am

lucky I don't have to ask to one day be

a marble or a walnut or a seed a beetle rolls

accidentally into a ball. I could tell you anything

I want—my sadness learned the trees

speak all the time without making any wind.

The Oriole

On the side of our weed-eaten driveway
my young daughter and I find an oriole's head. It's summer,
the world gone scared outside and in,

and the oriole's head part of all that confusion—
for now, the only part. The head
angled upward as though about to fly its absent body

out from the concrete, and the beak
splayed, lodging a silent squawk
toward us, this last moment preserved

like something from a crude museum an old city
would like to forget—a shriek,
my daughter thinks, shrouding the eyes

and softer parts of the head still missing.
This omen resting hard against the slab, as if in defiance
of becoming part of that uncarved statue.

Parable

The girl thinks of the cormorant, and the boy thinks
of the cormorant fisherman. The candy the girl

hands the boy is sweet, distilled with darkness.

The moon thinks of the cormorant, and the cloud
thinks of the cormorant fisherman. The moon complains

to the cloud about being drowned out by fire.

The tree thinks of the cormorant, and the rock thinks
of the cormorant fisherman. The leaves the tree

forgets on the rock look like little doorways lit.

The boat thinks of the cormorant, and the river
thinks of the cormorant fisherman. The boat lies

(the river is not handsome) gliding heavy from grief.

The fish thinks of the cormorant, and the rope thinks
of the cormorant fisherman. The strength the fish

feels in the rope is mirrored in the evening of the bird's throat.

The girl thinks of the cormorant, and the boy thinks
of the cormorant fisherman. The candy the girl

hands the boy is sweet, distilled with darkness.

Dream with Gun and Five-Year-Old Daughter

Hours before the divorce was final, the day

the divorce became final, I woke, knowing the dream

I had just dreamt could not be touched, the dream

in which my daughter took the form of a half-dog,

half-human, the dream in which my half-dog,

half-human daughter did not know she was dying

and had to be put down, her slow, slow dying

unable to interrupt her continuous smile, her *Like this,*

Daddy? as she tried to make me laugh, her *Like this,*

Daddy? though she already had been shot

to stop her suffering, her body calming, already shot

in the dream that real hours later became the day.

A Perfect Machine

Alone, in the dark, I wanted nothing more
than to talk with an actual person

full of problems similar to though not exactly

like mine. A recorded voice
provided several options while the hotel's TV

blared German images against an eggplant wall.

It was all I could do to choose a number.
Among others, the cathedral in Cologne

made me cry. This is something

I might have said to you, since you
are an actual person, not a perfect machine.

Or I might have said that once,

too late for a train, we ate croissants
with the tiniest chocolate hidden inside them

and the loud people walked all around us,

for hours, saying nothing, and saying everything
at the same time.

The Boy and the Boy Looking Back

The boy says, to the mirror, *I am good, I want*

to be good, I am good, his mother hurrying him to school
before her work, his father dead from not being good

to his heart, the inevitable weight, the boy knows,

of his whole life ahead of him, how the boy will be asked
and then no longer asked to make choice after choice

until they stop feeling like acts of free will but instead

like rivulets exposed in cracked river stone. It will be
up to him, he knows it, or it won't, and which was it,

when he killed the squirrel with a pellet gun, when

he regarded the dull eyes like holes cut into dusk,
the fists stiffened, seemingly, for whatever would come

next? *I am good, I want to be good, I am good,* he says again,

but the mirror says nothing back. The boy learns,
from this, the shape his one face makes. From this,

the boy learns he can outrun anything but that shape.

Fairy Tale in Which Wolves Are Housed in Shells

Then the villagers heard the howls only when holding the shells to their ears. So they dug from the wet sand greeting the sea as many opaque chambers as their fingers could find, small geometries of rock stuck beneath their nails afterward for weeks. Nights the moon felt heavy outside their homes, the villagers passed around the newfound shells, taking turns to feel each distinct howl within their ears, for no logic foretold what volume or pitch a shape would make. Sometimes a whimper emerged from a conch. Sometimes a roar erupted from a clamshell. This evolved into a game said to speak to the listener's remaining length of life. Years passed like wind against a mountain. Babies were born, and elders grew back into the ground. Generations later, after playing the shell game one milky night, a young boy never woke again. It was said his abalone shell made no sound. Eventually the tradition wore off. Children began playing with sticks while their parents slid cards across tables. On moonful evenings, the villagers looked inland toward the forest, noting the fat absence of wolf howls they had read about in tales passed down. So one night when the moon turned mostly dark, they buried the shells below the trees so deep they needed their heaviest shovels. Then they slept like unexplored caves. They woke like waves, and fried potatoes with bread in butter. When the moon again became a bone-colored bulb, the villagers heard a wail through the windows. They walked outside in silence to see that everyone had walked outside. The sound didn't cease: What they heard was a child crying. They explored the forest but couldn't find wolf or child or shell. The cries were coming from a tree. The villagers eventually tried to sleep. The child cried all night. When later generations spoke of that evening, they said the wail was the sound a wolf makes without a shell. But they no longer knew which tree that night was weeping. Their children grew up enough to know this tale was one real thing that wasn't true. Their children grew up looking at the wood that shaped their walls as though it had something to say. But the wood never said a thing. The wood only spoke in circles.

In My Memory of Living Together

I'm listening to the vague distance of a marching band
warming up or dying down, it's hard to tell. This is the summer
people have been drowning from something in the lake, the summer

my daughter rides her bike like there's no such thing
as theory. The pecan pleases my mouth the way an absent noun
becomes an obsidian knife, the way a river offers only

hidden edges. The doctor says his daughter is studying
to be a poet, and I'm listening to the vague distance
of a marching band warming up or maybe dying down, it's hard

to tell. On the tile floor, the screw rattles like a tooth.
Resting on the deck, in the sun, the squirrel splays its limbs
as though waiting to fly. The dark television hovers above

your hospital bed the way a handsome door conceals
a bright room. Though we sleep, the trains do not sleep, or
we try to sleep, knowing the trains are not asleep. I'm listening

to a marching band warming up, dying down, warming up,
dying down. The candles smell so real I can barely believe them.
This year, the Christmas tree will look particularly gorgeous.

Announcement

Excuse me, but I must say a few words,
for the backyard Bradford pear has finally bloomed
on this day, the nineteenth of February, a bright
Thursday afternoon. Here, where weather
avoids dramatic change, the seasons shift more subtly,
though this morning's graveyard now glows,
crowded with store-bought color. Mostly music
escaped the radio then, the occasional voice thick
and content with these local conditions, so I
kept driving, even when the empty school bus
slowly passed, full of silence. I don't know too much
regarding trees, but as for the beautiful foliage of spring
you may have read about in Buson or Walser,
the Bradford's white blossoms, those small breaths
swollen for just a few faint weeks, are the only evidence
the backyard ever sees. So I trust you will understand,
when, not too far from now, I'll have to write
of the cows huddled under the oak's shade
like calm statues, of the train engineer's excitement
while directing freight through the sleeping town,
of my feet beginning to numb in the clear river, needing
to pee but needing also to stand very still.

Prompt

A poem about silence without using the word "silence."

A poem about the last time you spoke with a squirrel.

A poem in which each concrete noun begins with the same first letter
as the nearest verb.

A poem that provides universal healthcare.

A poem in the shape of a wacky, inflatable, arm-flailing tube guy.

A poem in the shape of a tornado.

A poem that replaces each adjective with a warm cup of soup.

A poem about death whose only noun is "shoes."

A poem in the voice of a boulder covering the entrance to a cave.

A poem featuring a monochromatic color scheme.

A poem titled "Lines Written in an Empty Bathtub with the Lights
Turned Off."

A poem that breaks the fourth wall.

A poem whose AC runs too cold in the summer, whose furnace runs
too hot in the winter.

A poem with a small, potted succulent resting on its surface.

A poem in the key of E minor for an audience of smiles.

A poem offering 0% interest.

A poem that begins with the last words your co-worker ever said to you.

A poem whose lies are completely honest.

A poem whose number of lines could mean something significant.

A poem in the voice of how you think you should sound.

A poem about a river without using the word "river."

A poem that usually wears a size large T-shirt in black.

A poem that can be harvested for energy.

A poem that begins with your mother's last living breath.

A poem with the highest burning point.

A poem in the shape of the sound of thunder.

A poem in the shape of an octopus.

A poem in the shape of a wind turbine undergoing maintenance.

A poem that forgets the rule of thirds.

A poem in the shape of a committee proposal for allocating more
    funding to schools.
A poem titled "Embryo" in the shape of a cashew.
A poem about joy written with the keyboard's left side.
A poem made from fair labor.
A poem that ends with brushing its teeth.
A poem in the voice of a dialogue balloon hovering above your
    elected representative.
A poem that needs regular feeding.
A poem whose truths are all made up.
A poem titled "Poem" in the shape of a poem.
A poem in which your apartment is surrounded by a humid
    continental climate.
A poem the size of a quark.
A poem that ends by metabolizing attention into capital.
A poem presented in a triadic color scheme.
A poem that hands a stranger a cool glass of water.
A poem about silence without using the word "silence."
A poem whose last line isn't repeating the first line.
A poem in a voice saying anything real.

Communion

I went looking for silence but found words—

slabs of highway waterlogged from last night, houses
surrounded with thought. This morning, before light,

I spoke in a dream about hearing what no one should
hear, about running under sky the texture of wheat. Asleep,

I learned a beginning happens only once, though our hearts
refuse to listen. Asleep, I learned a beginning and an end

need something in-between—the gray lake empty
except for some clouds. Your poem about loss changed

nothing. Years ago, the night ice closed the roads, I walked
in thick stillness for pizza behind a bright window

where families laughed in a language I didn't know. Later,
wine-heavy, I strolled around that suddenly colder quiet

to smoke among the trees' frozen branches so I wouldn't
have to sleep. But here, in the car, there is music with no

words. There is desire without resolution. On both sides,
everything is green, everything is loud. I hear it all, clearly.

While You Lie in the Hotel Bath

Cold, air conditioner humming, looking

through an anonymous window, below me,

where layers of hot concrete cover

ancient soil, a train takes hidden materials

to be made into obvious objects

bought, perhaps, by people who work

in the surrounding high-rises, or eaten

by those driving their tiny cars along

these wide, model avenues, so that all of us,

some down there, others up here,

may regard the few transplanted trees,

green and thick with this gray morning,

like the soft, controlled explosions

we need them very much to be.

Advice

Damp silence following a late-spring rainstorm.
Fireflies' green staccato above the darkened lawn.
My small daughter, unwilling to admit she's tired, asks

if we can catch one, wonders what we will do with it
if we can. We live in the same imperfect world, she
and I, this imperfect world like the evening beneath

wrinkled sheets, this world in which we both understand
we are to die, like the firefly, like the grass, and *That's OK,*
she tells me, *Daddy—that's OK.* It's supposed to rain

again tomorrow. Maybe it won't. Overturned
on the table, the empty jar between us, its held air
swollen with what could have been our words.

Study Beginning on a Bedroom Ceiling

The way the wooden beams slope down
from the home's divided center;
the way the fan hangs untouchable, still,
a display from some future museum;

the way the elaborate curtains hide
the yard behind the house from eyes
too focused on an old book about everything;
the way the grass was once green, now

saturated with night; the way there is no moon;
the way the train's whistle interrupts
the quiet of cicadas' static; the way it is early
October in Texas; the way the child sleeps

heavily in the next room, nowhere near
the particular moment; the way the moment
is now inseparable from the child,
the child inseparable from the ceiling.

A Story about Death

Before bed, my young daughter wants a story, she tells me,

so I start by saying this story about death never ends, and though

my daughter must sleep soon, I promise to tell as much

as I can, this story that will continue within my young daughter

all her life, this story about how another little girl wants to know

what death is because her father died when she was seven.

So the story begins: the little girl whose father died

sets out from her house in the woods to ask, *What is death?*

She's ready to hear the answer. She's ready to say hello. She's ready

to know the dark, the same dark that now surrounds her father.

*

During her walk through evening oak and cedar, the little girl

notices the old woman's house, the living-room light squared

against the grass. The little girl knocks and begins to count;

when she arrives at twenty-five the old woman opens the door,

invites her in, motions to the three-cushion couch on which

the old woman had been reading a book. *Hello, old woman,*

the little girl says, *can you please tell me what death is?*

Death, says the old woman, *death is what a dog looks like when it visits the human world. Thank you,* the little girl says,

but I think you are wrong, and now I must keep walking.

*

The little girl feels the old woman's lawn damp beneath her feet

and thinks of the middle-aged man down the path who waved

last week while resting from his sawing of the wood. At this hour,

though, there is no sawing of the wood, the house so dark

the little girl recalls once watching a large animal whose sleep

was of such beauty she wondered if the large animal were dead.

But the large animal was not dead, so the little girl peeks into

the backyard, where the middle-aged man stands smoking

while regarding the silence of the trees, the small speck of sun

swelling and fading like a lightning bug in front of his face.

*

Why are you here, the middle-aged man asks the little girl

who responds, *Hello, I want to know, what is death?* The sound

of wind hurries through the idea of leaves. The moon barely

disrupts the sky. *Every time I try,* he says, *to think about death, all I can see is a bowl of oranges, just a blue bowl of bright*

oranges. Who lives here with you, the little girl wants to know,

so the man leads her in through the back door, flips the light,

points like a guide to the framed photos lining the walls.

All these people, I loved, they loved me, all dead, the man says.

The little girl sits on the green stuffed chair to rest a while.

   *

I'm sorry about these people, but I must keep going, she says,

and farther down the path, a forest clearing catches her attention

because one large tree occupies the otherwise empty field, not an oak

nor cedar, but a tree with twisting knots like knuckles, a tree

the little girl has never seen. *Excuse me, large tree, I need to know*

what death is, but no one can tell me. She hears only the whoosh

of an owl before settling into silence. *Large tree, you try on death*

every winter, how does it feel? A cloud interrupts the faint moon

as a small branch falls at her feet, a branch, when held, whose limbs

wishbone toward her chest and the space the owl made into its own.

   *

In whisper, she catches, *But you try on death every night.* She cannot

place the source of the sound, for within the tree's crown everything

is still—only her attention moves. *I shouldn't speak to what can't*

be seen speaking, she says, *but I think you know something I don't*

about death. Along the same darkened path she has been traveling,

a small brown dog trots without a glance in her direction, deeper

and deeper into the dark up ahead, where the forest again swallows

the path. *Death,* the large tree weakly breathes, *death resides inside*

us, and you, little girl, you are looking far away. I am not talking

to a tree, she says, *because all I hear is the wind, the wind, the wind.*

*

When the little girl steps toward the undiscovered dark, the owl

flies quietly from the tree until it can no longer be seen,

somewhere within that swollen grove. Entering, the little girl

feels like a stranger in an unfamiliar home in the middle

of the night; when she tries to find a light switch along the wall

all she touches is tree bark. Not knowing the way back from forward,

she continues the only way she can, her outstretched hands

scanning the space ahead, until glimmers of diamond-sized light announce a pond whose surface suspends the fragments of moon

glimpsed through the thought of the imperfect copse overhead.

*

Standing at what the little girl understands to be the water's edge,

something small and soft brushes against her leg, but she is unafraid

when she hears the small dog lapping darkness from the pond,

when she crouches to rub the dog's coat along the ribs, when

the dog stops drinking to lick her palm with a heavy tongue. *Nobody*

can speak about death, the little girl says. *Small dog, do you know—*

will it hurt? Was my father in pain? From above, the owl's vowels

punctuate the dog's breathing. Brief wind scatters the flecks of moon

across the black. *Death is not about pain,* the small dog says,

I feel pain every day. Even right now, she asks. *Even right now.*

*

You didn't answer my questions, the little girl says, *and I can't see*

you, even. The small dog wanders away from the pond, pausing

on the unlit path. *Yes, your father was in pain,* the dog says.

Yes, little girl, it will hurt. Something the size of a frog splashes into the water. In the distance, a substantial bell rings deeply,

then rings again, and then again, a slow pulse of roundness

that settles into the air the way wind presents itself as nothing

but fact. *I must go,* the small dog says, *but you need to know*

that death resembles most the pillow you prefer over all others,

that when you rest your head, you won't even think to be scared.

    *

Alone by the pond in the dark, the little girl decides to walk home,

for she has heard enough about death for one night. *The end,* I say,

but though my young daughter yawns, she tells me she is hungry

for a snack, and do we have any cereal, and she would like

an orange, too. In the kitchen, at her small table, my daughter

peels the rind into a plastic bowl, the underside of each piece

white as paper. As I pour milk over her cereal, she asks me

if the little girl in the story was me, or was it her, and I tell her yes,

I was the little girl, and I tell her yes, that she will be the little girl

one day. *Tomorrow,* she says, *I think I will be her tomorrow.*

2

Scrubbing the Skillet,

I realize my daughter just turned seven and doesn't know

I was seven when my mother crept into my carpeted room

while I played a video game to say my father, who had been

far away taking fluids from tubes in a California hospital,

had died. My daughter doesn't know I said *OK* and kept

playing so my mother would leave, so I could feel

how it felt not to have a father, or how having a father

who was dead was supposed to feel because I already

knew what not having a father felt like. Now, my daughter

doesn't know I can hear her cartoon spilling from the TV

as I finish the dishes, doesn't know I am building the scene

I imagine unwinding inside her mind, the one where she

helps the town children rope their runaway mare scared

and stuck in the mountains, even though my daughter doesn't

know how to ride a horse. But in this scene, if someone

were to tell my daughter her father had died, she'd know

to calmly walk the mare back all the way into town, whispering

into the animal's ear how pretty she was, how sweet, because

most nights, beside my tired daughter in her dark room

as she curves against sleep, that's what she whispers to me.

What You Think about While Your Neighbor
Is Talking to You in the Front Yard

The wind carries continuous weather
which always feels new. The wind
stirs a small smell, one you barely recognize
from childhood. But the wind
which you think you hear

is not the wind. That's the wind
disturbing what you think
you know: a branch, its leaves,
your neighbor's bulky brown coat.
This makes you question your senses.

Standing in the wind feels
like your body is moving
toward a place it will never reach.
You like the sound of this.
And you like the sound

of the wind as it rattles the tiny bones
in your ear. You like all of this—however
large, however small—so much
you don't know how to contain it.
The wind brings to you these feelings

you could never share with your neighbor.
He's still talking about something
not entirely specific. But you need a shower,
news you must soon deliver no matter
how much he believes in both of you.

My Sound Story

Listen closely. Here is my sound story. It begins,
like most things do, with waves and rain and thunder.
Do you feel you know me yet? Is there a connection?
What if I told you that crickets are not too far behind?
In autumn, all of this matters, how that morning egg resembles
any other morning egg, so I hope you are listening.
Do you hear the butter crackling? Do you hear
that utensil scratch the cast iron? These are important
parts of my sound story, as are those birds, outside
but near enough to hear. I imagine them singing
for each other, flying from branch to branch, which
I realize is the plot of many cartoons. So I lift
the skillet, slowly, since it is heavy, and I slide
the egg onto a plate and wait, as we all are waiting
now, for you to salt and pepper and eat it,
because eating an egg is silent, and to believe
this, like most things, we must see for ourselves.

Gold Country

A hummingbird circles a hummingbird
circling a hummingbird feeder.

//

Settling into my breath, I think that I
would not like to think so much, so often.

//

Oh, just a couple of horses clacking
their hooves across the street,

//

the riders deciding between them
what to do for an inevitable dinner.

//

Dripping from the tree, the sweetest plums
the ones punctured with little beaks.

//

Some coughing off in the hilled distance.
Some coughing off in the hilled distance.

//

My small daughter, knowing few words, clearly
speaks at the sight of the midday moon.

//

Room only for these thoughtless marks—
                            an impossibility.

//

A friend's voice on the phone, a doe
grazing among a gang of turkeys,

//

the back lawn sunburned brown—
the shade I'm sitting in enough.

//

Rows of choreographed cherry trees,
lines of black sprinkler heads between.

//

Slowed by beer, I watch late afternoon
gather around the house from this couch.

//

Centered in front of my face a vase
whose black-eyed Susans' petals droop

//

onto some fading Shasta daisies—
I wipe sweat from my forehead as I write.

//

Quaking aspens' shadows' fragments blot
the dirt trail within the parking lot's earshot.

//

I peek in the room to see my daughter sleeping;
rolling waves recede inside the sound machine.

//

The moon illumines cold living room tiles—
the loud house steeped in overnight quiet

//

while I read of Chinese rivers, mountains—
a sudden fly searches this vastness.

//

Unwrapping the cellophaned sandwich, I tear
a green slip of tape saying, *Enjoy more. Worry less.*

//

A noontime rooster in abstract distance
trying to return this warmth to morning.

//

A life spent looking through windows
                    instead of at them—

//

I cannot not watch
                    the deer feeding out back.

//

Rounding a curve, I swerve to miss
two geese slogging across the hot street.

//

While everything adds to the moment's singularity,
I have to give only each dark mark.

//

What's all this beautiful talk
but a plum flaunting its bloom?

//

Searching for rocks, my daughter and I
walk along the dry creek bed

//

flanked by faded grass, heavy oaks,
the kind of quiet silenced by sudden wind.

//

The strawberry seed stuck between my teeth
a secret I stroll around the neighborhood with.

//

A month of monotonous sun, finally
a gray day relieves the grass a jackrabbit

//

travels through in a distance marked
by that vast absence of movement.

The Way to Work

A billboard asks me
if I can name five types of apples.
I am listening to classical radio.
Suddenly, I am driving past the graveyard
and realize I can name only two:
red and green. So naturally I wonder
what, exactly, is wrong with me.
The DJ says there have been explosions
at the Boston Marathon. That's it.
The graveyard is now gone. Too far
behind me. Stores are trying to sell
office supplies, but they are fooling no one.
Now back to the music. The sun
all around. In ways I cannot touch
and in very gradual increments
somehow brightening the day.

River Oblivions

    a.

They are deciding whether the river should still be
called "the river." The trees anchoring the banks
rattle their leaves like shells, or like old money.
Evenings, the boy speaks to the river in the voice
of a flat stone thrown across the black, but the river
only knows the platitude of "continue." The girl stacks
the book on wind above the book on trees, but where,
she wonders, should she keep the book on silence?

    b.

They also need a new place
to park, tentatively titled
"The River Lot." The mayor
sews closed a backpack
full of stones and stops
walking in the rivers's mud
for the very first time.

With a pen whose clip
is an engraved pelican's beak,
the girl writes amendments
to having heard of the river
in a way she has not seen
it, when she has seen it.

    c.

On a sunny bluff overlooking everything, the town

holds an open vote on the river's name. The boy holds nothing
but a smooth, flat stone. The girl feels the currency

in what she reads while approaching the microphone to speak

clearly as water. Always, they have already decided. Crossing
what was formerly "the river," the wasp thinks the wind

is the kind of friend who spends his whole life leaving you.

The Living Need Light, the Dead Need Music

Having opened your book about Egon Schiele
(your apartment, alone, late morning, green tea)
I stare at his rough lines in order to understand
your mind, in order to know exactly what you do know

and what you don't: the dishes done, the orchid very close
to death, my crossed feet anchoring the coffee table,
the bedsheets still ruffled though mostly covering

the bed. Somewhere along these seasonal streets
you lead your children on bike to the park whose waterfall
I've never seen, while here the miniature big top remains
unmoved, heavy, its open flap framing a small mess of toys

so still they're speaking. I've long thought I knew about love
most everything, but water will mimic the shape
of its container, and the painting, no matter the subject,

is always only about the self. Later, when we regard
your soon-to-bloom peonies from separate vantages,
in one mind (calm, clear, watching for highway carrion)
a countered ant maps a path only the other mind can follow.

Still Life with Elementary School

Some time after the naughty child left
the imprinted ghosts of her soapy hands

all over the bathroom mirror,

the principal's intercommed voice became
a night river mangled through a dam.

The voice said, *Not this time.* The voice said,

No more. But the girl drawing a pear
gently at her desk said, *Yes, it is awfully sunny.*

The Pond

You were ready to drop some acid, to watch me eat pecans,
but I needed to ask you something about love
that I hadn't already tasted, that I hadn't even considered

could fill a room. The ducks floated in front of us
while the sun lit my face through rain-mangled branches.
I knew then that later, on the drive home, I would listen

to the song that always makes me cry, the song
without words but full of feeling, full of birds, full of the weather
we couldn't ignore for long. But there, in the partial shade

near the unnatural water, all we heard was the sound of people
talking along the trail while we walked around a thing
worth keeping warm. So, we said it. Then we said it once more.

The Fountain

There, he knows the quiet palmetto leaves by touch,
the way they curl back into themselves as quickly
as glass, and, in so knowing, presses between thumb
and forefinger a delicate edge. Once, when the land
lacked human conversation, a fox stalked a meadowlark
from the tall grass, wind the only proof the world
moved. He was not there, then, when the fox lunged and
the meadowlark flew like smoke from an extinguished candle.
He was not there, then, when the fox clawed apart
the meadowlark's chest, the pebble of its heart still beating.
Space, like time, he thinks, *is as corporeal as digging in dirt,*
and, when saying this within himself, remembers as a boy
in the field uncovering a squirrel's sudden skull. The sound
of water shimmering in the fountain is a sound he no longer hears
except when he is not there. But he is there. There he is.

Thirty Years

My clearest memory as a boy: upon waking, mistaking

my father's hallway shadow, unaware

how our house's midnight interpreted the faint

kitchen light. Another: in line to view

his casket-framed body, I thought I would cry,

but I didn't. Now I can't remember what

I saw and wonder, in those dulled days before,

three states away, his heart barely working, his mind

reportedly gone, if the cold confused him—

the sheets mere symbol—while the window offered

only the June sun bleaching the streets, the mountains,

the nearby beach. I imagine his aged face

would resemble a photograph of a distant sand dune

defined by wind. I even imagine being

there, bedside, holding his glass of water, reciting

Yes, yes, I do know who you are, as if staring into

a patinated mirror just to see myself saying it.

On Break

in the classroom where she teaches, she
eats Wheat Thins, washes them down

with V8. His phone tells him autumn

there is forgiving: the tree-lined river
idles past both kinds of ghosts they believe in.

Leaves pasted to the sidewalk, burned edges

the only evidence of seams. The poet
they're reading whispers about a lover's hair

in a book whose flowers are too specific

to be named here, where the river is full,
where one dark snake divides it.

Dream with Bird and Two Bloody Teeth

Of course my life feels out of control

because it is, so the clarion moment my front tooth

felt loose, I tore it out, my tongue rubbing the shard of tooth

I missed, so I stuck my fingers back in to pull the broken

bit I couldn't get the first time, the larger piece broken

almost whole against the paper towel, somehow knowing

next to wiggle the shrunken molar from its socket, knowing

then to smile in the mirror because even the magpie remembers

its reflection, but all I saw reflected was the way the room remembers

air, so I held both teeth in the vastness of my outstretched hand

opened for you and asked, *Can we live a real life? Does my hand*

look heavy? Over what does the magpie have control?

Essays on Idleness

Animal Idleness

The cat's jaw breaks awake inside this house dark with humidity.

Anxious Idleness

Those birds always sound so beautifully useless.

Audible Idleness

Morning wanes when the first word emerges.

Autumn Idleness

A sudden flood of thunder, or a squirrel runs across the metal roof.

Bag-Packing Idleness

One book on loneliness, two of haiku, sifting through your dream, sifting through your dream.

Barney Idleness

Singing with his soft, purple mouth, "What would I do / without my teeth," I wonder what he would do.

Carrot-Cutting Idleness

Right then, slicing those things, listening to some early Monk, I was worried only about technique.

Cheese-Grater Idleness

I should look at you before I look through you.

Choking-Hazard Idleness

Must bite into my food to taste it.

Cinematic Idleness

The antagonist realizes he is not the kindest human being alive on this dying planet.

Collage Idleness

I'm still trying to make this window a calm, cloudy square.

Conditional Idleness

There is even a patio where she sits, in her free time, to watch the birds filling up the empty parking lot.

Conversational Idleness

"I can't remember what I'm saying," you say.

Culinary Idleness

Whenever the microwave's rotating tray derails, it feels like my life's approaching its abrupt end.

Decorative Idleness

A quilt can be hung on any wall, like this.

Definitive Idleness

The grayer the sky, the greener the tree, the greener the tree, the grayer the sky.

Domestic Idleness

My black cat looks up at me like she doesn't know what a poem is.

Evidential Idleness

Illustration: I walk to the stairs so I can walk on them.

Excited Idleness

Infomercial: Only ten minutes left.

Exhaled Idleness

That quiet song of my bones growing strong before becoming brittle again.

Fabled Idleness

The moral, of course, is a horse at the pet store.

Gubernatorial Idleness

The neighborhood dog applauds the vintage sun inaugurating the end-of-work-hours lawn.

Hospital Idleness

She slowly tries the stairs that tried to slow her.

Hotel Idleness

While I read the plum-colored curtains' folds, the parking lot fills with rhetoric.

Ideological Idleness

This is a drawing to prove that clouds still exist.

Ill-Advised Idleness

Under the obvious weather, obviously under the weather, under the oblivious weather, obliviously under the weather.

Insomniac Idleness

Lately, I've been watching a single ant's speck crawl outlines on the wall, lit by the room's only lamp.

Interrupted Idleness

I trust the mail will soon appear in my mailbox, so I listen.

Kitchen Idleness

A thin sheet of Brussels sprouts' leaves lying left over in the sink.

Layered Idleness

A mind to thank the mind that thinks to thank the word for a word we do not see.

Lucky Idleness

For example, earlier this evening, when the phone rang, I just let it ring.

Marginal Idleness

They were deceiving the ocean, Mary, they were deceiving the ocean!

Middle-Age Idleness

If you prefer, pretend this isn't happening.

Morning Idleness

Sprinkling oats over my yogurt, I hope this one life stays about average.

Observational Idleness

The land moves under the weather and the weather moves over the land.

One-Way Idleness

I spoke with him the other day, by which I mean he spoke to me.

Parental Idleness

The black plum we pass between us, spilled juice the grass gladly absorbs.

Parental Idleness (2)

We killed the morning watching cat videos.

Pastoral Idleness

The field a field I'm standing in.

Patio Idleness

The dog calmly pisses into Buddha's open palm.

Produce-Aisle Idleness

The intercom recites the specials from somewhere in the ceiling too bright to be noticed.

Radio Idleness

This is your island of sanity. (Thanks for listening.)

Reflective Idleness

I say my name into a mirror, watching myself watch myself.

Remembered Idleness

I reach for the pencil behind my ear, but it's not there.

River Idleness

The field stretches like an endless trampoline.

Roadtrip Idleness

"Are you hungry?" "No, are you hungry?" "No."

Scenic Idleness

Fog pressed between the flexing remainder of trees.

Silent Idleness

The tiny spider descends from the ceiling like a parachutist.

Similitude Idleness

He's like one of those statues made to look ancient, surrounded by plants at the hotel pool.

Socratic Idleness

According to the overcast voice on the radio, everyone knows trucks are cheaper in the country.

Solipsistic Idleness

A poem may not help anyone, not even its poet.

Stevens Idleness

That the pear would house a pit rather than its seeds.

Suburban Idleness

An ad from inside a newspaper rides the air across a residential street.

Surprised Idleness

Reading this overly elaborate novel for two odd hours, I've been sitting on a shard of the bluest crayon.

Terrified Idleness

All over the wet morning lawn, bamboo shoots had sprouted loudly overnight, already knee-high.

Textured Idleness

Just a bit of hamburger dropped hot onto the carpet.

Transitory Idleness

The hope that a bus will soon be here.

Tree-Climbing Idleness

The farther I was from ground, the more I lived with a particular guilt.

Unabashed Idleness

There is no apology here, and there is no apology there.

Vita Idleness

I was born when people talked about the weather, and then I died when people talked about the weather.

The Living

I was ten when I locked my father's college ring
inside my dresser's wooden drawer to hide
his death from my friends who wanted to know
how it happened. Now, the ring's tissue-wrapped

in a basement box mixed with family objects
my daughter might one day choose to donate
and I've said *heart attack* a thousand times and one.
After thirty years of thinking, I don't think

my father didn't love me. I'm not sure what the living
understand about love. When my daughter grew
fearful of finishing third grade, she asked how
not to be afraid, so we blessed with our bravery

one of her forgotten rings she then wore to school
on the index finger she used to show me something
worth seeing, like the face she once found
among burls grown into the trunk of a bur oak.

3

A Natural History of Rivers

1

You wake up, it's still dark out, and the river's there behind you, back in your sleep, quiet as stone, flowing the opposite direction of your eyes. You name the river the same name you once named your daughter. Or perhaps the river was already named what you once named your daughter. You call to the river. You call to it by name. The river won't stop moving and answers only with a snake that's floating along its surface. But the snake disappears. The river encourages such disappearance.

2

You wake up, it's still dark out. In front of you the river is climbing the bedroom wall. On the river's bank, there is a little boy riding a bicycle. He stops to regard the river by watching it, but instead sees something in himself he doesn't like. The river has made a second moon. The boy grabs a stone to throw into the river, but you say *Stop!* The boy sinks stone after stone into the water. You tell him to look at what he's doing, and he says he can see what he's doing, that's why he does it. Then you tell him not to see. You tell him to try listening.

3

You wake up, and you call out *Charlotte!* You imagine a dry riverbed glimpsed by lightning. You splash water on your face, and in the mirror, there's a dry riverbed. Through the window, a dry riverbed. On your wall, a dry riverbed framed as a painting. There, in the painting, the sun's out. A bald eagle roosts in a tree. A little boy rides a bicycle along the bank. *Agnes!* you call out. *Simone!* You can't remember the name you gave your daughter. *Are you there, Lethe? Gertrude!* From your bookshelf, you find the book about riverbeds. It's called *A Natural History of Rivers*. You open the book. Each page looks the same. *Wait, Sam, is that you?*

4

You can't sleep, so you start the documentary on rivers. It's called *Snakes and Clouds.* The only light in the living room is the aura your television makes. Your curtains are drawn, but anyone walking outside at that hour would see the opposite of sleep. The film never shows the narrator, but you hear his voice. It is the voice of a submerged stone. On the television, a man is in a wooden boat. A single torch lights the way. The man sends a cormorant into the black water to fetch a fish. The flame feeds off the lack of wind. On the television, a boy skips stones along the surface, wishing to stand on the opposite shore. There is talk on the television, talk about how to channel a river. You recognize the sound of the submerged stone. The voice is familiar because it is your voice, a voice you have not heard in some time. The voice tells of the naming of rivers. That's when the doorbell rings. On either side of the curtains, the only light that glows is from the documentary.

5

You open the door, and there is your daughter. You remember the faint moon weaving itself along the water's surface. You can barely make out the distant shore. You invite the river in. *Have you missed me?* she says. You point to the television screen. You point to the sudden moon. All you want is to say your daughter's name, but your mouth won't open. With both of your hands, you hold out a blue quilt.

6

In the documentary, the narrator speaks of damming rivers. The narrator explains the ecosystem, the narrator explains displacement, and then the documentary cuts to a montage of men shouting about floods and electricity. The straighter the river's course, the more speed. The river's right there in your living room. She's beside you on the couch, cuddling a blue quilt. You've made popcorn to share, and you each take turns monotonously placing piece after piece in your mouths. It looks like you are eating tiny clouds.

7

You wake up, and it's light out. You put the kettle on for some tea. The sun shines like a far-off television. Through the window, you can make out even the trees on the river's opposite bank. A linden, a birch. A bald eagle nesting in a cottonwood. Someone's fishing, his body shortened by the water. In a letter, you write *Dear Agnes*. You cross it out and write *Dear Simone*. You have forgotten the kettle until it trills like a flute. You seal the envelope and carefully write the address for the moon.

8

In the stage play, there are two rivers, and the two rivers share the same name. You play one river. Your daughter plays the other. A stagehand pulls the curtain, and the audience is quiet as a cave. You say your lines perfectly. A committee of faceless men wearing gray suits stands on stage, and you are telling them about what happens under your surface. You are telling them about how you smooth stones like the wind. Your daughter stands next to you. She has somehow crafted a windowless room. The room surrounds her. It is invisible. But she can't see past the transparent walls. She sings a song she's spontaneously making up, and to ensure she's happy with each word, she keeps starting again from the beginning. She sings of the moon resting in the sky like an unbroken egg. She sings of growing tall enough to touch it. The song is called "The Cormorant." At the end of the scene, you're supposed to submit to the committee a photograph of your daughter's name. That's when your daughter will stop singing. In your wallet, you find a photo that says "Lethe." Your daughter continues to sing. On your phone, you find a photo that says "Charlotte," but again you hear the song's opening words. You find another that says "Gertrude." Another that says "Sam." Over and over, how the moon rests unbroken like an egg. Oh, to be tall enough to touch it.

9

You wake up, and you decide to make a painting of a river. For texture, you apply heavy brush strokes, and there are many blues, greens, browns, light grays. In the foreground, you paint yourself, and the figure of you looks directly back at you, as you paint. In the painting, you have a single right eye and two left eyes, one hovering above the other. The river is behind you, in the background. The river curls around the bluffs like the first letter in the word "snake." In the foreground, you are wearing a red shirt. You are wearing an orange wool cap. All your eyes are open. You worry over what color to paint the wind. You call the painting *Simone*. From a distance, you could be mistaken for a flame.

10

The river floods when you aren't looking, and when you are looking, the river also floods. The river washes homes away and swallows bridges. All the while, the river sings a song. It's about the moon hiding behind a cloud. You try singing the song too. The words won't come out right. When you try saying *moon,* what leaves your mouth is *stone.* You keep saying *thunder,* though that word is nowhere in the song. You feel like the smallest bird. The smallest bird fallen from the nest onto a sidewalk. The smallest bird suddenly surprised by air.

11

You open your eyes, and you're on the top floor of a natural history museum. Charlotte is on display. You know this because the label tells you. The diorama shows the depths of Charlotte's waters, the flora and fauna forever suspended underneath. While viewing the model river, you and your daughter hold hands. The caption on the other side says "Agnes," and you hear a nearby docent saying *Sam* this and *Gertrude* that. In the gift shop, you buy your daughter an enamel pin of a river. Eating ice cream in the sun on a bench, you ask your daughter about the exhibit. What did she like the most. She says she liked the thing that swallows a coin after spiraling in seemingly endless circles. Eating ice cream, she wears the river pinned to her red shirt.

12

You wake up, it's still dark. You realize your daughter has climbed into bed alongside you. She groans, complaining of growing pains. You switch on the lamp to softly read aloud from a book called *A Natural History of Stone*. Your daughter loves this book. Her eyes are closed. She is half asleep. Your daughter doesn't understand the book, which is why she loves it so. You read quietly. *In the beginning, there was a river. The river was blue as an indigo quilt. The river shaped the stone with its voice. The shape is always changing. The river has a single name.* This part your daughter especially loves. Her eyes are closed, but she tells you to read it again. So you read that part again.

The Clouds Here Are Beautiful

But the maps were all broken.
Neither he nor she could see much
of anything—duct tape fenced the windows.
Still, they looked for one single object:

a cassette tape, a peony, a mote of dust,
a penny, a popcorn kernel, a match, a whisper,
a bottle of whiskey. But no one said a word, not
one. The stars that night were Christmas lights

reflected in a turned-off television screen.
The moon, even, was barely there.

Great House

Because I rarely think of the word "pharaoh," when I hear it

humming in my head I have to check the definition but instead
remember fifth grade, Mrs. Huckabee, my blue shirt, that the word

in Egyptian once meant "great house." I hadn't known

until then a word could enclose something more than itself.
In the United States of America, in the year 2020, it's the month

of March—right before bed the government said everything

would mostly be fine, said all we needed to do was wash our hands.
But this morning when we woke as we wake every morning,

we could no longer leave our homes. I fed my dog a red potato.

I asked my daughter about myopia. I watched through the window
sunlight performing nothing in particular while the radio announced

if someone were to die, we could not hold a funeral. Then

for the first time in years, I wrote the word "pharaoh," learning again
whenever this happens, no matter what, I must first misspell it

before the letters begin making any kind of sense.

Fairy Tale

The student writes a word, "copse," quickly
realizing if the poem were read aloud, the listener
might assume the word is "cops" and become confused

because why would that small child in the poem
walk straight into an unlit murder of cops looking
for the owl she had been hearing all night, the owl

who had kept her from sinking into the lake
of sleep she had so badly wanted? Because

the student is talented, the student understands
"thicket" would also suffice, but those syllables
disagree with the poem's neighboring sibilants

and circular vowels, so the student begins to feel
the first light of uncaring, an unfamiliar feeling, knowing
"copse" is more true than "thicket," knowing that sound

allows a more important logic than sense. But class
raises its concern after the poem is read aloud

because the class feels compelled to police
sense in a way the student wishes to forget since
the student suddenly feels like the small child

looking in the dark for the owl who kept her
far from sleep, the owl whose ring-shaped offerings
may only be described in the act of voicing.

A Novel Written against Oblivion

begins with music—a man shoveling snow
has no way of knowing this time the steadfast snow

slowly refilling the path he worked to clear won't stop
until his heart stops first, the daughter writing the same story

inside their lamplit house, believing what she's making
to be make-believe, Crayoned snowbanks beneath two pines,

classical radio filling the room, the shovel's hard measure gone
cold. But this novel written against oblivion is not a story

about the man but a story about love: how the daughter
lets her dog outside, sees the father's crumpled frame

against white, pleads into the face she holds with her hands
before continuing to live a life in which she brings the dog

everywhere she goes after, until the dog no longer can be
brought to a place. Then this novel written against oblivion,

this story about love, explores the ghosts imprinted onto
the grownup daughter's mind: riding her bike through the clarity

of neighborhood air, all day wanting to dance to evening jazz,
the antique map of Texas drawing her far into sleep.

Without the dog, the daughter alone finds her way to yet
another place with trees and cicadas, another with hills and rivers

and clouds, another with birdsong each morning, her hands
darkened with garden dirt, because this novel written against

oblivion is really a story about love, and the daughter has maps
and music inside her. Far in the future, when the daughter dies,

for the daughter dies in this novel, too, it's still not a story
about death. It's written in the present tense, and the protagonist

is the daughter. When the novel ends, because all stories end,
the reader understands more about oblivion, even more about love.

There is no escaping the weather we can't live separate from.

The Park's Nearly Empty This First Week of Spring

Have I mentioned the crow slowly approaching,
the one making harsh sounds into the air
like a crow who knows what he wants
will only come to him by complaining?
You might say I have some time on my hands.
You might say this crow could be a kind of symbol.
Bless you—that I will have to consider.
That I should think about for a while.

The Swing Set

The first thing you texted me
that Sunday morning I stared out
at thirteen inches of snow, the snow
I piled into conquerable hills

rising from the corners of the yard
forgotten, that Sunday morning
the dog warmed the silence
of my bare feet so I could see

the neighbor's maple buds
marooning the off-white sky
and regard the foolish desire, foolish
even this lonely time of year,

for color—when your name
brightened the phone's cracked screen
the first thing you texted was
I dreamed you asked me to write a poem

about a rusty swing set. Later that Sunday
morning I remembered the image
from the sad film you stopped
watching in which two characters

are driving through upstate evening
snow to the boyfriend's family farm
when the girlfriend looks into
the passing bleakness to find

in the empty expanse sprawled
before a long-abandoned homestead
the absolute redness of a gleaming
swing set. That Sunday morning

I didn't text you a description
of something that cannot be
found. I said *Now you have to write it.*
Maybe you are. Like love, that

sudden rush of color out of nothing
but inertia, offered here—
I can give you this. I can give you
that. I cannot take anything away.

Equations

The trains of San Marcos are pretty.
The trains of San Marcos are occasionally loud.
The trains of San Marcos carry a certain amount of dignity,
not so much where you feel uncomfortable,
just enough to demonstrate a pleasing level of confidence.
The trains of San Marcos enjoy *Monday Night Football*.
The trains of San Marcos sometimes seem small.
When they were young, the trains of San Marcos learned to spell
before any other trains could spell.
But the trains of San Marcos are addicted to eBay.
But the trains of San Marcos support local gatherings
such as rallies, bake sales, watering the community garden.
The trains of San Marcos were valedictorians.
The trains of San Marcos group their errands together.
The trains of San Marcos work hard.
Somehow, the trains of San Marcos are sad.
Sad because they know you can hear them
while you hum a catchy tune to yourself.
The trains of San Marcos don't recognize the song.
The trains of San Marcos make their own music.

Extravagance

I have been waiting. I have been waiting

all day long. A pair of running shoes rests
inside a small box cushioned inside a larger box

taped and staying very still inside a truck.

And a woman wearing monotone shorts and sneakers
is driving, and as you may have guessed

by now, she is listening to a classic rock station

because her employer allows such extravagance.
As for me, I am listening to my own expectation

of the engine to soon vibrate these clean dishes.

Which is not entirely true. You see,
I am actually listening to the soft silence

stuffed into each room of this wooden house.

Of course the air conditioner clicks on
and then clicks off, and at some strange moment

I never can predict, it simply clicks on again.

The Suspense of Simply Existing

Caught first by surprise,
then allowing in just a little delight,
having noticed from the backyard

the hot-air balloon frozen in the morning sky,
a dollop of yellow paint flattened against enormous gray,
I was at last caught by terror, imagining

the cluster of astonished faces looking out
onto that hard, untouchable map
of which I was a most unnoticeable part.

Problems of Prose

Honestly, how annoying
to have opened the novel where I stopped last night
and not know on which page to begin
because of that double-sided bookmark.

True, tree limbs scratch around the house, cold
for this autumn's first time. And how quiet,
between winds, this empty interior—many pears
have perished despite the refrigerator's effort.

Weeks ago, the repairman said he could see
no problems, said everything should be working fine.
I wanted to share what I had recently read: "Listen—
we, too, are dying slowly." But he was the talking type.

Since then, I have been trying very hard
to trust his words, because I cannot trust mine,
because I fear there will soon be
no difference between them.

We Didn't Believe

Through the ceiling, where the holes were widest,

we watched the night sky as it passed,
placid and cold. To each other, we burned

like smooth horses. Though blankets
were not enough, listening

pleased the violence of our ears.

Fixed to the carpet, smelled the dark grass
of the fields, bodies still warm

with weather. The sky
a soundless face. We've heard

our mouths will taste like fire in heaven.

The Committee on Silence

One morning when the sun erased all the night's undoings, the villagers finally forgot how to close their eyes. They had grown tired of not seeing what all happened while they slept. They had grown tired of losing those fragile moments blinked away during each day's dazzlement. That morning, no matter how hard the villagers tried, their eyelids would not budge. Even the softest fingers could not pinch closed any neighbor's sight. They rejoiced. They would never miss the wolf approaching from the forest. They would never ignore the thief leaving the church with a sackful of eggs. They would never look past the child sticking chewed gum on a statue's eye. They rejoiced and named the day Apollo Day. The Festival Committee was appointed. The Committee employed workers to saw down trees to be fashioned into spiral staircases leading far into the sky. The Committee hired labor to weave the surplus of exotic textiles into a quilt great enough to be cloaked around the entire village's circumference. The Committee asked all the children to make with their hands a number of drawings to be nailed into each stair and stitched into every square of the fabric wall. When the moon next brightened its whole being, the festival was held. Music fled from mouths and instruments. Fire turned animals into food. Some people climbed into the night sky so far even eyes that could not close could not see them. Some people watched the wind move the wall like a single, continuous sheet of hymns. Some children hid and some children sought, but the children who were seeking always won. It was all anyone could speak of for the entire next year. The Committee decided on many agains. Festival after festival came and then went. After some time, the particulars gradually changed. Staircases were repaired, or replicas were made. The worn fabric was switched with nylon weave. Yet the children's drawings remained largely the same. The elders saw in these sketches what they remembered seeing when they would blink. Instead of stories, each year's festival ended with a sigh. The villagers continued their lives of light, speaking only of what they saw. The wolf approaching from the forest. The thief leaving the church with a sackful of eggs. The child sticking chewed gum on a statue's eye. Sometimes what they saw they no longer wanted to see. A test was run, and village experts concluded everyone's hearing had weakened. All signs pointed to it worsening. When someone spoke of a lake they once saw, the listener only heard a handful of silt. The experts decided there was nothing to be done. Year after year, the Committee continued to plan. One morning after the festival, when the sun lit the conquered dark, the villagers forgot how to open their ears. They had not planned for this. They named the day Harpocrates Day. No festival was to take place. They established the Committee on Silence. This brings us to the present day.

Without Your Voice This Evening

The way the peonies droop in the window suggests
they are nearer to death than us. It's been ten months

since I've seen you, and that same sun, again, is about to set.

I know, I know. Today, alone, more bodies innocent as trees
made their way into that world toward which we have only

gestured. Still, I can't stop searching for words to describe

this perfect loneliness: pomegranate, daffodil, turmeric, ant.
Still, I can't stop searching for words to perfectly describe

this loneliness: turbine, ghost, piano, lavender, eclipse.

A Story about a Story about Death

I am old. My grown daughter is helping me fall
asleep, telling me a story she once heard
as a little girl. My daughter is holding my hand
the way the ground holds a greedy shadow. The story
goes like this—a little girl's father lived
to be a cottonwood. Every day, the girl read books
entangled in branches. Evenings, the moon
swam between leaves. Interrupting the story,
my grown daughter nods toward the dark
window. In it, a soft painting of a child
caring for a tree. That's when I know
I'm asleep, pretending to be a white sheet
of paper. All around, June wind blows
the limbs' whispers like familiar snow.

Oracle

There was a lamp spilling light up along the wall.

There was a bird. There was a neighbor

scraping snow off the driveway. There was Schubert.

There was Liszt. I think the bird was black.

I confess, I did not see it. Still, it suggested to me

in a monotone voice that I should change my life. Oh,

also, there was a lake. And there were geese. The geese

I saw, I promise. There was a canvas bag heavy

with food for a party. There was not really a lake, I mean

it was more like a pond. This can be a little difficult

to distinguish. There was talk of pecans, and there was talk

of wine. I know this, because I could taste them.

There was a black bird feeding off entrails. There was sun.

It was not winter. It was not a river, either. The bird

casually mentioned I should change my life. The neighbor

was clearing the driveway of snow. I fell out of my habit

of answering the phone. Sometimes, it would ring and ring.

Yes, hello, there were metaphors everywhere, there

were even three pieces of pie. Always, there was more

to say. Spilled light on the ceiling. A voice's words

interrupting the music. There was a book by Agnes Martin,

a book by Jean Follain. Listen—there was a very black bird.

Change your life, it whispered. *Okay,* I whispered back.

NOTES

The epigraph is from Agnes Martin's *Writings*.

"The Oriole" is after Ted Kooser's "The Mouse."

"Fairy Tale in Which Wolves Are Housed in Shells" is after Gaston Bachelard in *The Poetics of Space* (translated by Maria Jolas): "Wolves in shells are crueler than stray ones."

In "Gold Country," the lines "What's all this beautiful talk // but a plum flaunting its bloom" are adapted from "Gathering Thorn-Fern" from *The Book of Songs,* and the phrasing "Settling into my breath" is adapted from T'ao Ch'ien's "Drinking Wine," both translated by David Hinton in *Classical Chinese Poetry*.

"The Living Need Light, the Dead Need Music" takes its title from the synonymously named short film by The Propeller Group.

"Essays on Idleness" takes its title from Kenkō's *Essays in Idleness*, translated by Donald Keene. The phrase "about average" in "Morning Idleness" is from Issa, translated by Robert Hass.

ACKNOWLEDGMENTS

Infinite thanks to the editors of the following publications in which these poems, sometimes in different forms or under different titles, first appeared:

AGNI: "Fairy Tale"
The Atlantic: "The Living"
The Believer: "Dream with Gun and Five-Year-Old Daughter"
Bennington Review: "Parable"
The Cincinnati Review: "What You Think about While Your Neighbor Is Talking to You in the Front Yard"
Conduit: "Some Circles" and "Oracle"
Copper Nickel: "A Story about a Story about Death"
Crazyhorse: "The Boy and the Boy Looking Back" and "In My Memory of Living Together"
CutBank: "We Didn't Believe"
DIAGRAM: "Fairy Tale in Which Wolves Are Housed in Shells" and "A Natural History of Rivers"
A Dozen Nothing: "Advice," "On Break," and "The Park's Nearly Empty This First Week of Spring"
Ecotone: "Essays on Idleness"
Fence: "Still Life with Elementary School" and "Dream with Bird and Two Bloody Teeth"
Great River Review: "The Fountain"
Gulf Coast: "Announcement," "Equations," and "The Committee on Silence"
Hayden's Ferry Review: "Communion," "The Pond," "The Clouds Here Are Beautiful," and "Without Your Voice This Evening"
Image: "Great House"
The Massachusetts Review: "Scrubbing the Skillet,"
Missouri Review Online: "Prompt"
More in Time: A Tribute to Ted Kooser (University of Nebraska Press): "The Oriole"
New England Review: "A Story about Death"

Pleiades: "My Sound Story"
Poetry Northwest: "The Suspense of Simply Existing"
Ruminate: "Problems of Prose"
Southern Humanities Review: "River Oblivions"
Third Coast: "Gold Country"
TYPO: "Study Beginning on a Bedroom Ceiling"
Waxwing: "The Living Need Light, the Dead Need Music"; "A Novel
    Written against Oblivion"; and "The Swing Set"
West Branch: "A Perfect Machine," "While You Lie in the Hotel Bath,"
    "The Way to Work," and "Extravagance"

Thanks also to the Poetry Society of America and Nuar Alsadir for
selecting several of these poems for the Robert H. Winner Memorial
Award, and to the Kimmel Harding Nelson Center for the Arts for an
Artist in Residence Grant.

ABOUT THE AUTHOR

Trey Moody was born and raised in San Antonio, Texas. His first book, *Thought That Nature* (Sarabande Books, 2014), won the Kathryn A. Morton Prize in Poetry. A graduate of Texas State University and the University of Nebraska-Lincoln, he has received the Poetry Society of America Robert H. Winner Memorial Award and his poems have appeared in *The Atlantic, The Believer,* and *New England Review.* He teaches at Creighton University and lives with his daughter in Omaha, Nebraska.

CONDUIT BOOKS
& EPHEMERA

OTHER TITLES FROM CONDUIT BOOKS & EPHEMERA

The Art of Bagging by Joshua Gottlieb-Miller

Thunderbird Inn by Collin Callahan

The Birthday of the Dead by Rachel Abramowitz

The World to Come by David Keplinger

Present Tense Complex by Suphil Lee Park

Sacrificial Metal by Esther Lee

The Miraculous, Sometimes by Meg Shevenock

The Last Note Becomes Its Listener by Jeffrey Morgan

Animul/Flame by Michelle Lewis